WOMEN HAVE POWER 40 POWERS THAT WOMEN POSSESS

VOLUME 1

ALPHONSO CRAWFORD

Copyright © 2016 by Alphonso Crawford

All rights reserved. No part of this book may be reproduced or transmitted in any form or by any means without permission of the author.

ISBN 978-0-935379-22-8

Library of Congress Control Number: 2016913230

Published by New Life Educational Services
P.O. Box 96
Oak Lawn, Illinois 96

Printed in the U.S.A.

Table of Contents

Introduction 1

1 A BIG MOUTH 3

2 ADVANCEMENT 5

3 LIFE 7

4 UNCONDITIONAL LOVE 9

5 WEAKNESS 11

6 ADVOCACY 13

7 COUNSEL 15

8 ENTREPRENUEURSHIP 17

9 SEX 19

10 BOLDNESS 21

11 CRYING 22

12 CHARM 24

13 SPIRITUALITY 25

14 GIVING 26

15 HONOR 29

16 SUBMISSION 31

17 FAVOR 33

18 INNOVATION	35
19 TEACHING	37
20 PRAYING	38
BOOKS BY ALPHONSO CRAWFORD:	40
ABOUT THE AUTHOR	42

Introduction

Women are powerful. Though often stereotyped as being weak, meek, emotional, and ineffective, this couldn't be further from the truth. A confident woman who recognizes all of her gifts and powers can become unstoppable in the workplace, in her personal life, and even in the spotlight. Remarkable things happen when these powers are unleashed.

In this book you will discover many of the powers a woman brings to this world. Though hidden at times, these powers exist in every female who has the courage to look for them. When women apply their patience, communicative skills, empathy, and power of counsel, they become a powerful vessel for change in their own lives and even for the good of mankind.

In the bible we often see how powerful women can become through the art of persuasion, for example. A woman's strength may not be obvious, and perhaps not in the form of physical brute force, but females have powers that can be far reaching and remarkably effective. One may think of female powers as fine chisels that operate gracefully where a mighty hammer would only inflict damage.

The powers of women represent age-old and time tested wisdom and tact that is now being verified through scientific study. This may finally be the era in which women may practice their unharnessed abilities without fear of judgment or censorship. Use your beauty and your softness to enable a voice that others will truly hear.

Women can take control of their own destinies when they allow their powers to soar to their full potential. These powers that must be used responsibly and thoughtfully. Defend your values, nurture together, and protect your future.

Use this book to rediscover and ignite your female powers. Then go forth and use your powers wisely and confidently to create love, happiness, and success for yourself and for those around you.

1
A BIG MOUTH

"And Moses brought their cause before the Lord. And the Lord spoke unto Moses, saying, "The daughters of Zelophehad speak right: thou shalt surely give them a possession of an inheritance among their father's brethren; and thou shalt cause the inheritance of their father to pass unto them." (Numbers 27:5-7)

Too often, women are characterized as second-class citizens in the world as well as the Kingdom of God. Women are encouraged to act submissive at times. This does not mean that they do not have an important and valuable role to fill. Women and their big mouth power are essiential.

A woman's big mouth power means they have the ability to influence others in a large way. With their powerful voices, they can establish authority and share vital messages, leading others towards what is good and right. Teach your flock to be faithful. Speak louder than the temptations that threaten to lead many astray.

Another task that requires a woman's power of a big mouth is the act of singing, praising, and rejoicing. In Jerusalem, the rejoicing of women and children could be heard from a distance. Their voices were so powerful that their joyful singing carried throughout the land. Use your voice to share joy.

Use your voice to cry out against injustices in the church and the world.

The big voice is important. Women speak righteously and it is essiential that everyone can listen and hear the information they share. Women are leaders and teachers.

The significant progress of many women today all over the world can be attributed to their big mouth, boldness, and willingness to stand up and speak right. God told Moses, "The women they speak right."

In the Old Testament, the daughters of Zelophehad, spoke up, challenged the status quo and claimed their inheritance.

You must use your voice to champion and protect what is yours. Do not allow yourself to be overrun in silence. Your voice gives you power to claim what is yours. Teach others to stay the righteous course and fulfill your destiny.

2
ADVANCEMENT

"And the Lord God said, it is not good that the man should be alone; I will make him an help meet for him." (Genesis 2:18)

Men are the head of the family, but women are ahead of men. Women were created to assist men on their path. It makes sense then that women would be ahead of men regarding life's journey. Otherwise how could they be considered helpful?

To be useful, women were created to be more advanced in some areas and they were gifted the power of advancement. Therefore they help men advance in life. Women were meant to act as advisors, therefore having more power than the men despite the fact that men were seen as having a more esteemed position. Men fulfill their roles often consulting their wives.

Behind the scenes, a woman has the power to advance her family through her role as a thoughtful mother and wife. When she nurtures the spirit of man, she advances the whole family and even the whole spiritual community. In the eyes of God, both men and women are equally perfect. A female can stimulate advancement through nourishment and encouragement, which becomes more powerful than the masculine technique of authoritarianism, as she inspires acts of faith and greatness. She exercises this power through hard work, teachings, and nurturing.

In this way, she serves God wholeheartedly by helping man become what God intended for him to be. This is an enormous power and responsibility. Not only can women stimulate the advancement of man and mankind. As the ultimate helpers, a woman holds the knowledge and power to advance in faith, at home, and in the workplace.

3
LIFE

Women have been blessed by God to fulfill His mandate on the earth. One of the powers given to them is the power to give life and sustain that life. Every individual in this world came in life through a woman and also was sustained by the woman.

The Woman Gives Life

"And God blessed them, and God said unto them, be fruitful, and multiply, and replenish the earth......" (Genesis 1:28)

The woman is to partner with the man to produce children. She is wired to accommodate mysteriously and feed the child in her womb for the duration of about nine months. Have you ever wondered why babies are so attached and endeared to their mothers? There is this natural affinity that both have for each other. (Isaiah 49:15) The women have been blessed, empowered and commanded to conceive, deliver, and nurse their babies; which is why they do these things effortlessly.

The mother is a life giver. She is an epitome of fertility and fruitfulness. Rebekah had the Patriarchs of two mighty nations in her womb. She gave life to them. Esau and Jacob came forth to fulfill God's agenda on the earth. (Genesis 25:22-24)

She Sustains Life

"She ariseth also while it is yet night, and giveth meat to her household and a portion to her maidens. She is not afraid of

the snow for her household: for all her household is clothed with scarlet." (Proverbs 31:15,21)

The children at home are closer to the mother, by default, except for any extreme reasons, that some more attachment with the father is developed. She is the home builder, the keeper of the home, a regular and one that creates that needed balance in a family.

Without her efficient coordination, there will be some conflict. There are many qualities in a virtuous woman that men lack and will never have because that isn't there nature. She is caring, hospitable, accommodating, and sensitive, an efficient planner, the family chef, mother, wife, adviser, etc. It would be inappropriate to compare children who never experienced the love of a mother to those who did. The woman is a steward and a caretaker of the lives that she helped to generate.

4
UNCONDITIONAL LOVE

Women have the awesome power of unconditional love. It is inherent within their nature, displayed within the family constellation all the time. That puts them in sync with God's salient attribute "agape love," the God kind of love.

"For God so loved the world, that He gave His only begotten Son, that whosoever believeth in Him should not perish, but have everlasting life." (John 3:16)

This kind of love brings:

- Resurrection
- Resurgence
- Revival
- Reconciliation
- Renewal
- Reciprocity
- Repentance
- Rest
- Rewards

- Restoration

- Resolution

God loves hard and he imparted this gift to women so that they can teach us how to love.

"....because the love of God is shed abroad in our hearts by the Holy Ghost which is given unto us." (Romans 5:5)

5
WEAKNESS

It might seem counterintuitive to list weakness as a power. While we know in our hearts that women are not weak, it is still a steadfast stereotype. Far too many people expect women to be weak and foolish. Herein lies the greatest power. Because there are people who expect little, it is easy to outsmart and impress them with a display of impressive strength. There is also additional power to be found in admitting and confronting our weaknesses. It is only then that we can turn them into strengths.

The misinterpreted weakness of women builds a dam behind which an enormous tidal wave of power swells. When the walls come down, and a female's true nature is revealed, the power becomes doubled still due to the element of surprise.

Don't be afraid to reveal your vulnerabilities. For when you show weakness, that is when you muster the most help. Being vulnerable can be umcomfortable, but it doesn't require shame or embarrassment. Everyone needs help at one time or another. When you do need help, say so. Then watch as many gather to support you. In this way, your expression of weakness leads to enormous strength. The power of one may be great, but the power of many is infinite.

Shared weakness is freeing and uniting. It can bring an emotional release of pent up frustrations, making you feel lighter. It can also lead to a new expression of peace and love. This happens when you recognize that your efforts to appear strong aren't as powerful as revealing your weaknesses.

Learn to transform your weaknesses into power. Don't waste time arguing that women are not the weaker sex. Instead, let their tendency to underestimate you become the gateway to surprising everyone around you. Let weakness be your source of strength, whether through misjudgments or collective action. For a woman, weakness can truly be powerful, a great advantage.

6
ADVOCACY

The world is full of injustice. The poor are oppressed. At times the most vulnerable are exploited and victimized. The kindest people are discriminated against. This can either be a source discouragement or one of empowerment. As a woman, you have the power to change this. Advocate for what is right and just.

Speak rationally and utilize the connections fostered through compassion and the maternal instinct. Promote the health and wellness of the people around the world, particularly children and other women.

When women ban together as advocates of a common mission, they become unstoppable in a powerful way. Work together to restore the greater good. Together women can achieve so much more than when they are alone.

Support the female leaders in your community. Too often women compete against each other and in the process tear one another down. When you build up your neighbor you fortify your own village. Advocate for all, and all will be lifted all.

Reach out to those who are suffering, or appear to be struggling. Offer whatever means you can and go further by advocating for their benefit. Break the cycle of poverty and selfishness. Build relationships and connections that will foster your mission. Ensure that the needs of those around you are adequately met. Don't forget to also advocate for yourself along the way. Ask for what you need. Speak up when others do wrong by you.

Speak and rally against all forms of oppression, injustice, or corruption. This is another way you can utilize your voice. Shout for social justice. Be an advocate not just for yourself and your fellow man, but for the will of God. Advocate for God by sharing His word. Reintroduce the righteous path to those who have strayed. Be the voice of reason.

7
COUNSEL

As you traverse through life, you have the power of counsel on your side. At times this counsel is referred to as Spirit, the Holy Spirit. Conflict or adversity naturally arises through the course of life, but you do not need to overcome these trials alone. You always have the power of counsel on your side.

You enact the power of counsel by sharing your troubles with your peers, or with God through the power of prayer. Even the most dire of circumstances have a way of working out with faith, trust, and good counsel. Taking up counsel both with the Lord and with your peers brings numerous benefits.

When you give your problems to God, you instantly recognize that you are not alone and the Holy Spirit is on your side. When you counsel with other women, you gain the power of their insight. Often, when going through a difficulty, we develop tunnel vision, wherein we see the problem but not all of the alternative routes. In counsel we share our problems and listen to the answers, either spiritually or in the spoken word.

The power of counsel brings a roadmap that enables one to make choices throughout life's journey. When you focus on the righteous path, you see the solutions more clearly.

We have to be willing to humble ourselves and share our problems with others. Women are also skillful at acting as counsel for others.

Women excel at using the power of counsel. They are communicative of their thoughts and problems.

They instinctively know that the answers we seek cannot always be found alone. Females assist each other in overcoming all odds when they work together through counsel and when they engage the Holy Spirit as their guide.

8
ENTREPRENUEURSHIP

Female entrepreneurs are now seeing faster growth than ever before. The economists agree, up until this point, women have represented an under-tapped force in the business and finance sectors. What does that mean? Women hold the power to economic expansion. Not so long ago, in 2007, women owned just 6% of all businesses. That number has skyrocketed to 30% in recent years, and the trend is still growing. Women throughout the marketplace are proving that they do indeed possess the power of entrepreneurship.

Women are also demonstrating that they have the ability to do more than less. Research shows that investors are less likely to entrust their funds to a female CEO, but this challenge isn't holding them back. Despite the fact that women usually start their businesses with less than half of the capital that men in similar companies start with, they are still proving to be successful. When costs are cut to the bare minimum, there is less waste throughout the organization making it more stable.

Some experts are even toting this decade as the golden age for female entrepreneurship as investors start to realize their ability to adapt to every challenge, turning setbacks into advantages.

Additionally, women are displaying a remarkable propensity for identifying and filling gaps in the current market, making the most of every opportunity. They are hustling to start new services, create new products, and sell to new segments within the marketplace, leaving no stone unturned. Women are famous for sharing this success. There has been an explosion of trainings and boot camps for female entrepreneurs around the country.

The success of women in entrepreneurship doesn't have to be a divisive factor. When the entire market is lifted through the empowerment of women, everybody wins. A woman's power of entrepreneurship improves business and society for all.

9
SEX

Perhaps the most powerful of female attributes is the power of sex. It is a power that takes a great deal of tact and discretion. Nonetheless, some women are unaware of this potent ability. Others abuse it, diminishing its effect. The power of sex is emotionally charged, especially for young ladies who are frightened by it and for mature women who have had negative encounters.

The female sex opens doors and melts the minds of men. Indeed, the thought and potential can indeed be more powerful than act of engaging in sexual intimacy. It continues for a short term after that, but diminishes over time. A man will do, say, or promise nearly anything when seeking opportunity to mate. Passion makes both sexes do foolish things, but in most of these situations the woman has the ultimate power. They always maintain the power to say "no." Men know this and endeavor to please a woman's sensibilities. Too many women cast aside this power carelessly.

The female's power is well known and researched in the marketing industry. Consider for a moment just how many advertisements utilize scantily clad females to grab your attention. The female form is a powerful image, particularly when her sexuality is on display. Meanwhile, most males would stop and assist a female in distress, whether young or old.

This is a responsibility ingrained in society. Males are compelled to protect and appreciate the female form.

A wife learns to motivate and nurture her husband through intimacy. This bolsters his ego and inspires him to go forward into the world and establish greatness, making the object of his affections proud.

The sexual attraction of a woman serves many purposes. It brings passion and pleasure to the human soul. In a contrasting point, sex attracts men to women and encourages them to stay nearby where the same female can assist their journey, helping as God intended.

10
BOLDNESS

"The wicked fleeth when no man pursueth: but the righteous are bold as a lion." (Proverbs 28:1)

A fearless and self confident woman will usually have a heart that is open and clear, and that's among the many things that tends to make her totally different from the norm. These women brighten up a room with their magnetic energy. The bold fearless and confident woman frighten the close-minded and inspire all those who have long hungered for tangible proof that they too will serve themselves well by igniting their passions and confidence.

These women push themselves because they understand that life won't wait on them and they have to go out and get it as they desire it to be.

These bold and confident women make their move. They risk getting the no rather than sitting on the sidelines. They have learned and are in the process of pushing forward. They don't wait for someone to bring them the opportunity they desire. This woman finds the way to go after life's dreams and achieve her goals.

Bold women are vulnerable, learning from their mistakes. And they keep on pushing turning challenges into conquests.

11
CRYING

"O Lord my God, I cried unto Thee, and Thou hast healed me." (Psalm 30)

"The eyes of the Lord are upon the righteous, and His ears are open unto their cry." (Psalm 34:15)

"The righteous cry, and the Lord heareth, and delivereth them out of all their troubles." (Psalms 34:17)

When you feel helpless in extenuating circumstances, crying brings great relief. Women release themselves right away. Men restrain themselves because of cultural norms.

The macho culture inhibits men. They must not appear to be weak. Consequently, many of them die prematurely by suppressing their emotions and converting them physiologically.

Women cry all the time as they experience a wide range of emotions.

- Crying is a discharge—you release any kind of anxiety, nervousness, distress, or bitterness you may have been holding.

- Tears rinse your eyes—they contain antibodies that fight against dangerous microorganisms and clean our eyes.

- Crying gets God's attention.

- Crying unwinds us—helps us to minimize the stress in our bodies.

- Crying helps us to get in touch with our feelings.

12
CHARM

"And it came to pass in an eventide, that David arose from his bed, and walked upon the roof of the king's house: and from the roof he saw a woman washing herself; and the woman was very beautiful to look upon." (II Samuel 10:2)

Nothing has captivated men more than the rise and fall of the flowing curves of women. To lose himself, all he has to do is to gaze into the depths of a woman's eyes.

Women hold men spellbound with their charm. Many men from all walks of life have bowed at the citadel of a woman's charm, sometimes to their detriment. We have witnessed this through all the scandals we have seen and read about.

There are women that have standards and will not use their bodies for exploitation and gain. Society mainly sees women as sexual objects. Most advertisements use the body of a woman to sell products.

Women use your charm to glorify God in your body.

"Know ye not that ye are the temple of God, and that the Spirit of God dwelleth in you." (I Corinthians 3:16)

13
SPIRITUALITY

"And it shall come to pass afterward, that I will pour out my Spirit upon all flesh; and your sons and daughters shall prophesy, your old men shall dream dreams, your young men shall see visions." (Joel 2:28)

"And the same man had four daughters, virgins which did prophesy." (Acts 21:9)

"Then He answered and spake unto me, saying. This is the word of the Lord unto Zerubbabel, saying, Not by might, nor by power, but by my Spirit, saith the Lord of hosts."

(Zechariah 4:6)

I have been around so many great women of God that left an indelible impression on me because of their spirituality. I was touched, challenged, encouraged, supported, and went to the next level because of their tremendous spirituality.

"And the angel answered and said unto the women, fear not ye: for I know ye seek Jesus, which was crucified." He is not here: for He is risen, as He said. Come see the place where the Lord lay." (Matthew 28:5-6)

"And I entreat thee also, true yokefellow, help those women which laboured with me in the gospel, with Clement also, and with other my fellow labourers, whose names are in the book of life." (Philippians 4:3)

14
GIVING

"And it came to pass afterward, that He went throughout every city and village, preaching and showing the glad tidings of the kingdom of God: and the twelve were with Him. And certain women, which had been healed of evil spirits and infirmities, Mary called Magdalene, out of whom went seven devils. And Joanna the wife of Chuza Herod's steward, and Susanna, and many others, which ministered to Him of their substance." (Luke 8:1-3)

Now this is wonderful. Look at the devotion of these women who had been delivered and healed by

Jesus. When the Lord delivered Mary Magdalene, her life would never be the same. She was completely transformed into a fully devoted follower of Jesus Christ. The same is true of Joanna and Susanna, whether they were possessed of demons or had severe diseases. The Lord delivered and healed them, and they became zealous followers of Jesus.

The reality is that ministry requires money. In fact, Luke 8:1-3 tells us that Jesus' own traveling ministry which involved preaching, teaching, healing/helping people was funded by a group of women in particular, some or all of whom had been helped by Jesus. After listing these names Luke 8:3 says: "These women were helping to support them out of their own means."

This passage of scripture says they, "were contributing support out of their private means." As Jesus and His disciples traveled around announcing the glad tidings of the kingdom of God, they would need food each day. They would need clothes if their own wore out. They might have need of an inn to stay in at times. So, these women who had been blessed by the power and grace of Christ did what they could to bless Him. They gave of their private means. Now, we don't know about the financial status of Mary Magdalene or Susanna, but we are told that Joanna was the wife of Chuza who was Herod's steward. That is truly amazing! A true disciple of Jesus Christ lived within the palace! Joanna's husband was the man who was in charge of all the King's vast estate. No doubt Chuza was a very wealthy man, who lived in luxury and ease in the palace. But now that the Lord had intervened in Joanna's life, and set her free from oppression and disease, she had no other goal but to simply follow Jesus and serve with her substance.

The problem with money is that it is sensitive and a personal thing for many of us.first of all, for many people, money is their God. It represents power for some, social status for others, pleasure, control or a combination of all these things for others. Money equals livelihood and its not easy for us to part with.

But as David prayed before the people to God in

I Chronicles 29:14 in regard to the resources that he and others had given for the building of the temple:

"Everything comes from you, and we have given you only what comes from your hand." Before this he prayed: "But who am I, and who are my people, that we should be able to give as generously as this?"

These women that Luke observed probably couldn't think of anything better to do with their money than to make sure that the Saviour and His disciples were provided for. I believe that these women went to the local market in each town that Jesus visited, and bought food each day. Then they would probably cook it and serve Christ and His disciples each day. Take on the chore of washing their clothes. They would provide monies if they needed to stay in an inn. There was no obligation. This was glad service born out of love. Folks, that is how we should all serve the Lord. The Lord doesn't want our grudging service. He wants hearts on fire with love to serve Him out of joy!

David understood everything comes from God, belongs to God and giving to the work of God is a gift, a grace and responsibility. Paul called upon the Corinthians to excel also in the "grace of giving." Giving is a grace (a gift) God gives us, it is a privilege. It is not to be viewed as a burden. Jesus is recorded as having once said: "It is more blessed to give than to receive."

The greatest, most secure "investment" you can make with your money that also produces the greatest "dividends" is in regard to the work of God. We are to give because God is a giver by nature. In fact, perhaps the best known verse begins by saying: "For God so loved the world, that He gave…" And God gave His only, His all, His best!

You cannot out-give God. Go ahead and try.

Now, did Jesus need these women to provide for His needs? Absolutely not! God says that, "every beast of the forrest is mine, the cattle on a thousand hills (Ps 50:10). The Father would have provided for His Son, even in miraculous ways if necessary. But Jesus accepted the service of these women that they might demonstrate their love and affection for Him.

Women, Men, as we serve the Lord, He is giving us an opportunity to demonstrate our love for Him.

15
HONOR

According to I Peter 3:7, the woman deserves honor, it says, "Likewise ye husbands, dwell with them according to knowledge, giving honor unto the wife, as unto the weaker vessel, as being heirs together of the grace of life; that your prayers be not hindered." To further buttress this point the Bible instructs men to love their wives unconditionally as Christ loved the church (Ephesians 5:25). To love means to care, to cherish, and to respect. These four habits are synonymous to honoring a person. God planned the best for women, but it is up to them to be able to receive such honor.

There is a place of honor for every woman who cares to position herself appropriately. I Peter 3:1-6, which are the previous verses of our opening scripture quote, stresses on the wives being Godly, submissive, and modest. That means that honor isn't cheap but must be earned, so not everyone deserves it, and not all can have it. It is the exclusive right of virtuous women. When there was a need in heaven to birth a Saviour into the world, a woman of virtue from the genealogy of Jesus was necessary, and Mary was deemed fit. The Bible never actually said much about her lifestyle and person, except that she was a virgin; she had kept herself pure and usable by God.

There is no better scripture than Proverbs 31 when talking about women and virtue. Verses 10-11 say, "Who can find a virtuous woman. For her price is far above rubies. The heart of her husband doth safely trust in her, so that he shall have no need of spoil." The virtuous woman is priceless she cannot be compared to anyone or substance, this is honor. The trust of the husband for her is from his spirit and not based on external factors; this is full regard and honor. While it is impossible to love and respect a person you don't trust, it is so easy to love and regard someone that you trust

To further stress the importance of virtue, verse 25 says; "Strength and honor are her clothing: she shall rejoice in time to come." The Bible relates honor to virtue. Just like such a woman puts on her clothes, it is the same way she wears honor, so it follows her everywhere and all the time. It isn't conditional. Women of impeccable character and personality attract honor to themselves by default. They don't beg for it or manipulate people for it. It flows for them naturally. Her husband regards her with honor, and that is why he can fully trust her with just anything, whether he is present or absent. Verse 28 says that her husband and children praise her. Can you see the man beating such a wife or talking rudely to her? That isn't possible. The way to honor is by being godly, modest,and submissive. Honor might seem expensive, but it will pay you to multiple dimensions in the long run (verse 25: "...she shall rejoice in time to come."

16
SUBMISSION

The male and female differences between persons of both genders might be too pronounced in many instances, giving much of the power and privileges to men, but you can't take anything away from the females. They have absolutely nothing to lose as God created them that way (Genesis 1:27, 5:2), so He did a perfect job. The world's system is one that functions opposite to the plans, purposes, and principles of God Almighty (John 1:10-11, 14:22, 15:19). It tries to bring them to the same level. God did not intend for women to Lord it over the men, not that they should even be at the same level, but to be submissive to them (between spouses). For Him to have designed it that way means that it is ideal.

In Ephesians 5:22-24, it says "Wives submit yourselves unto your husbands, as unto the Lord. For the husband is the head of the wife, even as Christ is the head of the church: and He is the Saviour of the body. Therefore as the church is subject unto Christ, so let the wives be unto their husbands in everything." When Christ rules, the church submits; when He instructs, she obeys. The same hierarchy should exist in the home. While it may be hard to submit to a harsh, insensitive, selfish, and ungodly man, God's Word never changes, it still says, "submit." This instruction wasn't meant to afflict and subjugate the women but to empower them. For that is the only way that they can manifest their strength and dominion.

Women are divinely packaged to exercise their control by submission just like Jesus (John 10:17). The only way to their throne is first by bowing down. In Ephesians 5:25, God instructed husbands to love their wives unconditionally.

Notice that the instruction to the women came first before that of the men meaning that the way to earn the respect, admiration, and favor of a husband is first by submission. No sane man would choose not to love a submissive wife, and when your husband loves you unconditionally like this you become his queen. It makes you the center of his focus, he cares for you, anyone who challenges you, must first go through him. The church has dominion because we are submissive to Christ, so he bestows on us that authority. Please note that this isn't a call to mischievous or exercising submission for an ulterior reason but obedience to a Biblical injunction.

When God wants to deal with the family, He relates to the man directly because he is the head. The husband is supposed to pass the details to the wife, and she is to obey ("For the husband is the head of the wife, even as Christ is the head of the church…")." Whenever the wife goes beyond her place to receive instructions, or ideas or to chart a new course, it will always result in a disaster because that is the job of the man. Eve broke the ranks, and women are suffering from the consequences (Genesis 2:21-23). Adam was the one God asked not to eat the fruit and not Eve, but she listened to the devil and attempted to instruct the man with a new direction. Perhaps if the serpent had spoken to Adam, he would had resisted because he heard directly from God. The only way women can have the best, release their might and potentials, be loved and cared for, is by submission to their husbands.

17
FAVOR

"That our sons may be as plants grown up in their youth; that our daughters may be as cornerstones, polished after the similitude of a palace:" (Psalm 144:12)

The scripture above refers to the daughters of Zion, and every woman or girl in God's kingdom, irrespective of age is included. It portrays them as being conspicuous, beautiful and admirable; such that they are envied by other men and women outside of God's kingdom. The furnishings of the palace are nothing short of grace and excellence. They are polished means that they shine: God's glory and favor cloth them. It is noteworthy to reiterate that this is beyond the outward appearance of women or the attraction that culminates in sin and perversion. This piece is all about the radiance and the beauty of heaven in a woman that makes her indomitable, unstoppable, irresistible, and charming. This glory flows from her spirit and has nothing to do with her physical body (I John 7:38, I Peter 3:3-4).

"And the Maiden pleased him, and she obtained kindness of him, and he speedily gave her all the things for purification...." (Esther 2:9)

"...And Esther obtained favor in the sight of all that looked upon her". (Esther 2:15). "And the king loved Esther above all the women, and she obtained grace and favor in his sight more than all the other virgins; so that he set the royal crown upon her head, and made her queen instead of Vashti" Esther 2:17.

"And it was so that when the king saw Esther the queen standing in the court that she obtained favor in his sight; and the king held out to Esther the golden scepter that was in his hand. So Esther drew near and touched the top of the scepter" (Esther 5:2). We can see the hand of God upon Esther that made her become the queen and preserved her despite all odds. As many virgins as possible were collected from the whole empire, she was divinely predetermined to be loved and cherished by King Ahasuerus above all others. This one goes beyond bodily beauty, or tribe, or background. It transcends all logical and natural explanation, it is simply supernatural. Ruth also experienced the favor of provision and marriage from Boaz (Ruth 2:14-20, 4:13).

The favor of God on a woman isn't for a selfish agenda but to propagate the plans and purposes of God. It must benefit the people of God. "...And who knoweth whether thou art come to the kingdom for such a time as this?....and if I perish, I perish" (Esther 4:14-16). She never hesitated to risk her life to rescue God's people from imminent destruction. She was placed in that position because of this assignment to preserve the Jews.

The last thing about this favor is that it requires a passion for the Almighty and His people. Ruth denied her idol Gods and her nation to follow after Jehovah and Naomi, her mother-in-law. "...thy people shall be my people, and thy God shall be my God." She moved from poverty, widowhood, and frustration into the lineage of Christ by the oil of favor, which was because she followed after God and His people.

18
INNOVATION

Innovation means the tendency to invent something new. It also means for one to be creative, to be full of good ideas which will benefit other people. This quality was displayed by some women in the Word of God. I t shows us that women have so much ingenuity and creative instincts.

"Then cried a wise woman out of the city, hear, hear: say I pray you, unto Joab, come near hither, that I may speak with thee. Then the woman went to all the people in her wisdom. And they cut off the head of Sheba the son of Bichri and cast it out to Joab. And he blew a trumpet, and they retired from the city, every man to his tent..." (II Samuel 20:16, 22). This account narrates about a wise woman who delivered her city by her wits and boldness. They were presumed to be hiding a wanted villain, an enemy of the state. So the whole city was under serious threat. The monarch, military generals, and the men of that town took cover due to fear, but a woman of substance, courage and innovation stood to rescue them by her wisdom. She knew that she was endowed, and she made use of her gifts at that critical moment.

Innovation, as discussed in this context, is one that benefits others and humanity. It is neither selfish or self seeking. A charming woman in Joppa, Dorcas was full of good works, she had polished the lives of many such that her innovative deeds became the reason for which God brought her back to life

(Acts 9:36-42). The iconic virtuous woman of Proverbs 31 is another excellent example of one wielding the power of innovation. "Who can find a virtuous woman? For her price is far beyond rubies..

And worketh willingly with her hands...She considereth a field and buyeth it with the fruit of her hands" (verses 10, 13, and 16). From here we see that a woman of innovation is one that is efficient and hard working. She makes plans and executes them with the proceeds of her hands. Lastly, it takes the Spirit of God to be innovative, so endeavor to be connected to Him (Job 32:8).

19
TEACHING

To teach means to instruct, guide, and persuade an audience or person. The people instructed understand and are ready to take a new course of action. Some women in the Bible displayed this attribute.

Women are the primary teachers of children, especially during the formative years. And probably the greatest teachers.

Mary instructed her son Jesus and the Bible says, "And Jesus increased in wisdom and stature, and in favor with God and man." (Luke 2:52)

Priscilla instructed Apollos, a great orator. (Acts 18:26)

Marva Collins and Mary MCcloud Bethune were some of the greatest educators of the twentieth century.

There are some attributes in women that makes them great teachers. They have the care, concern, patience, tenderness, and intuitive traits that men lack. Their teachings changed lives and impacted destinies.

20
PRAYING

"Who through faith...Women received their dead back to life again..." (Hebrews 11:35)

One of the inherent powers that women possess is prayer. The quality in them that inspires them is their grave concern and resilient nature to the issues of life. You can see this spirit in them painted graphically in the scripture above. Everyone can attest to how impossible it is to cry, persist and pray a corpse back to life. There is just something about the praying woman that draws virtue (power) from heaven; it is the resilient and dogged faith that emanates from their spirit. There is nothing more precious than a prayer mother or wife.

In II Kings 4:1-37, the Shunamite woman displayed an incredible spirit of faith and prayer that was later used as a reference in Hebrews 11. She refused to give up on her dead son but pressed her way to victory. Her faith sparked up something in Elisha, God's anointed prophet. "And when she came to the man of God to the hill, and she caught him by the feet, but Gehazi came to thrust her away. And the man of God said. Let her alone, for she is vexed within her.... And the mother of the child said, as the Lord God liveth, I will not leave thee. And he arose and followed her." II Kings 4:27-30. Her faith stirred up the faith of Elisha, and she even refused to go until she had gotten her desire. What most men and fathers would give up on, the women and mothers will hang on until they break through to their desires.

There is another cogent illustration highlighted in Mark 7:25-30. The Syrophenician woman demanded healing from Jesus for her daughter and was refused, but she remained adamant. Jesus said He wasn't sent to her and her nation but Israel. This faith filled woman replied in verse 28; "And she answered and said unto Him, yes Lord, yet the dogs under the table eat of the children's crumbs." This woman never minded being called a dog, as long as that would be a pathway to realizing her desires. That was another instance of the power of a praying woman.

There are many praying women today who have stood in the gap for family, friends, and many others that needed prayer in rough circumstances and witnessed the miraculous working power of God.

"Praying Women" is God's divine design. Every woman that prays with passion and faith wields incredible and indomitable power.

BOOKS BY ALPHONSO CRAWFORD:

CROSSROADS: POEMS ON RACE/LIFE/POLITICS

TWO HEARTS: LOVE POEMS AND LOVELETTERS

LIFE' WAY UNTIL: POEMS ON FAITH/HOPE/SALVATION

WISDOM: 25 FACTS ABOUT WISDOM

TRIUMPHANT: 25 WAYS TO EXCEL IN LIFE

100 WAYS FOR PEOPLE TO GET HEALED

VOLUMES 1-4

WOMEN HAVE POWER: 40 POWERS WOMEN POSSESS VOLUMES 1-2

CATHEDRAL OF PRAYER CHURCH AND PRAYER MINISTRY (773) 419 2205

"Watch and pray, that ye enter not into temptation: the spirit indeed is willing, but the flesh is weak." (Matthew 26:41)

"Therefore I say unto you, what things soever you desire, when ye pray, believe that ye receive them, and ye shall have them. And when ye stand praying forgive, if ye have aught against any; that your Father also which is in Heaven may forgive you your trespasses. But if you do not forgive, neither will your Father which is in Heaven forgive your trespasses." (Mark 11:24-26)

"And He spake a parable unto them to this end, that men ought always to pray, and not faint." (Luke 18:1)

"Be careful for nothing: but in everything by prayer and supplication with thanksgiving let your requests be made known unto God. And the peace of God which passeth all understanding, shall keep your hearts and minds through Jesus Christ." (Philippians 4:6-7)

ABOUT THE AUTHOR

Dr. Alphonso Crawford is an Apostle of health and healing. He is the pastor of Cathedral of Prayer a church without walls. Dr. Crawford received his background in biblical studies at Moody Bible Institute. He holds the B.A. from DePaul University, the Master of Divinity from McCormick Theological Seminary, the Doctor of Ministry from Chicago Theological Seminary respectively at the University of Chicago.

www.ingramcontent.com/pod-product-compliance
Lightning Source LLC
Chambersburg PA
CBHW072041060426
42449CB00010BA/2386